DEAR READER,
THANK YOU FOR BUYING MY BOOK!
YOU CAN ALSO BUY AND READ MY FIRST BOOK ABOUT BLOCKCHAIN TECHNOLOGY

YOU CAN FIND IT HERE.
SCAN THIS QR CODE

Contents

Introduction

What is cryptocurrency? Bitcoin, Ether of Ethereum, Litecoin and many others are cryptocurrencies. They have had a lot of publicity, Bitcoin in particular, and are being increasingly accepted as money.This ever increasing acceptance has created a boom in the dollar value of cryptocurrencies. It is true to say that cryptocurrency is a type of money. However, before we begin to describe what cryptocurrency is, we need to answer a more fundamental question and that is the following.

What Is Money? Money is fascinating in its own right, it has existed in various forms throughout the history of the human race. Money has two main features that are; it is a means of exchange and it is a store of value.

What is a means of exchange? A means of exchange is something that most people are prepared to accept, in exchange for something of true worth. This might be their labor, their goods, their home or something else.

What is a store of value? A store of value is something that is accepted as representing the value for something of true worth. This could be something as suggested in the previous paragraph.

If any type of money is to execute these roles, it has to be trusted by those that use it that it is able to fulfill these functions. In the past, there have been all sorts of money. Salt, beads, cattle, silver, and gold are but a handful of examples.

All this is leading to our first question, which was," *What Is Cryptocurrency?"*

Cryptocurrency is money that is created, using the encryption techniques of advanced computer programming. By use of these techniques, funds are transferred and the transfer is verified. Cryptocurrency is digital money.

It is possible to create cryptocurrencies that are independent of governments and central banks. Such currencies are decentralized in the way the inventors intended them to be. When we look at the history of cryptocurrencies, we shall see that such independence was a major driver in the creation of cryptocurrencies.

A number of central banks have found great uses for the underlying technology, but any resulting currency not be cryptocurrency, as envisaged by its original creators. Any such currency coming from governments or banks will be centralized and the original creators of cryptocurrency were completely opposed to such centralization.

A term that will be frequently used in this book is *fiat currency*. The people involved in cryptocurrency call the currencies we use, in every day life, 'fiat'. Using this definition, we can say that dollars, euros, renminbi, yen, pounds and rubles are fiat currencies.

Chapter 1: A brief history of Cryptocurrency

The history of cryptocurrency is very recent. Some think that Bitcoin was the first electronic money. This is not actually true, as electronic means of exchange have been with us for a while. Most people are familiar with EFTPOS (Electronic Funds Transfer At Point OF Sale). Eftpos began to be used, throughout the world, in the early 1980s. The currencies involved were definitely fiat.

Something called the *Electronic Mall,* began in the USA and Canada in 1984, which provided a form of ecommerce via computer networks; this was followed by the first Internet ecommerce application called *CompuMarket.* At this time, the World Wide Web did not exist, however, after its inception in the early nineties, ecommerce really took off. *Amazon* was formed in 1995, *eBay* and *PayPal* followed in the late nineties.

All of these depended on fiat money, however, during the 1980s, further development was taking place in digital money. In the early part of that decade, David Chaum, an American cryptographic expert, proposed the use of cryptography in financial matters. He became involved in a system called

DigiCash, based on cryptography. This system, although it failed, paved the way for, what was to follow in digital cash.

In 1998, someone called Wei Dai described an anonymous distribution electronic cash system. His idea was followed by that of Nick Szabo, which required users to complete a cryptographic *proof of work*, a concept vital to cryptocurrency. This all leads up to Bitcoin, which was the first cryptocurrency and is still the most successful. On November 2, 2017, the value of one Bitcoin exceeded $7,000 (US)!

Bitcoin's early history: Bitcoin was invented by someone, with a Japanese name, Satoshi Nakamoto. On October 31, 2008, Nakamoto published a white paper on Bitcoin whose title was,' *Bitcoin: a peer-to-peer electronic cash system,*'. The motivation for this form of money was the near collapse of the world financial system in 2007-2008.

In January 2009, the first Bitcoin was minted or *mined.* At first, only Satoshi and Hal Finney, a brilliant programmer deeply involved in cryptocurrency, transacted in this currency, to get away from what they saw as intrusive government surveillance.

Initially, one Bitcoin was valued at less than 0.002 of one US dollar. This was the cost of electricity needed to mine it! How times have changed, with the value of one Bitcoin in November 2017 exceeding US$7000!

There is no one who has ever seen Nakamoto; there are many who believe this name is a pseudonym for a different person or perhaps a group of people. There have been a number of outings of Nakamoto, but all have proved spurious.

The whitepaper showed how cryptographic techniques would make possible the creation of electronic money. The first block of 50 Bitcoin, named Genesis, was mined during January 2009 and the first transaction, using Bitcoin, took place between Nakamoto and Finney. The value given to one Bitcoin in late 2009 was less than US$0.002. This was the value of the quantity of electricity required to mint one Bitcoin, with a desktop computer. A significant feature of Bitcoin is that it is impossible for more than 21,000,000 to be mined.

An important part of the history of Bitcoin took in May 2010 when a Florida programmer transferred 10,000 Bitcoins to someone else, who lived in California, so he could buy two pizzas, costing US$25. Today those pizzas would be valued atmore than US$70 million.

In August 2010,a hacking involving Bitcoin occurred for the first time. The hacker found weaknesses in the system so that he or she was able to generate 184 billion in BTC. At that time in June of 2010, the value of 1 Bitcoin (BTC) was about 1 Dollar, however, it fell to near zero as publicity about this disaster spread. This incursion and the finding of other vulnerabilities, combined with the discovery by the government of how money laundering could be done using Bitcoin caused serious problems.

Despite this, Bitcoin's value continued growing and by November 2010 the f Bitcoin's capitalization was more than US$1 million for the first time. One Bitcoin had staged a comeback, from its low of August, to a value near $0.50 US.

In January 2011 there was a lot of bad publicity for Bitcoin about its use on the Silk Road, which was a dark web market place for all sorts of illicit activities and things, such as endangered species, drugs, child porn, and other contraband for untraceable transactions. Despite or perhaps because of this the value of Bitcoin continued to rise. In February 2011 it reached parity with the US dollar. Years passed, and by March 31st 2013, Bitcoin had a capitalization of $1 billion US.

All crypto currencies need an electronic wallet in which to put the electronic coins. In June 2013 25,000 BTC (US$375,000) was hacked from a wallet. Later that year in August 2013 a federal judge presiding over a case stated that Bitcoin was money. There were other developments in 2013, in November the first Bitcoin ATM opened, and Bitcoin received the blessings of Federal Reserve Chairman Ben Bernanke, who many say, saved the world in the 2007-2008 recession.Unfortunately, this acceptance in the USA is not necessarily mirrored in other countries, where transactions in Bitcoin are often prohibited or restricted.

Most of the news in the Bitcoin world in 2014 was positive but not everything. Mt. Gox, one of the largest Bitcoin exchanges went into bankruptcy. This disaster was not caused by a flaw in the blockchain concept, which underlies most cryptocurrencies. It was caused by a small software error that had not been spotted. Human fallibility more than anything else caused this problem.

2015 was generally a good year, although there was a continuing controversy about BTC transaction speed leading to the creation of a new cryptocurrency, called Bitcoin Classic, in a technical transformation called a *fork*. We will say more about this later.

Other cryptocurrencies: The sincerest form of flattery is being copied. The success of Bitcoin has led to a huge number of other cryptocurrencies. In November 2017 there were more than 1,250, with new coins being launched every day. Most of these coins will not probably last into the future. Most cryptocurrencies use the technology of Bitcoin, called blockchain. Some don't use blockchain but most do.

Ethereum: Ethereum is the number two cryptocurrency by market capitalization? Is Ethereum a copy of Bitcoin? NO!!

The most significant thing concerning Ethereum is that rather than just money it is a platform by which applications using blockchain can be devised. This is the main reason for the amazing success of Ethereum that has seen its value rise from $8.24 on January 1, 2017, to over $300 in early November 2017.

The early history of Ethereum: A clever young Russian called Vitalik Buterin, proposed Ethereum in a whitepaper that he penned in 2013 at the age of only 19! He was born in 1994, and in 2000 his parents moved to Canada from Russia, for what they saw as better opportunities in Canada than Russia.

During Vitalik's school years, it was obvious he was very talented in mathematics and computing. His father who was a computer scientist taught Vitalik about Bitcoin. Vitalik was fascinated, seeing the great potential for blockchain, far more than its monetary use in Bitcoin.

After he had written this paper, he left the University of Waterloo in Canada to work on Ethereum all the time. At the beginning, Ethereum only had a core of four people, including Buterin; development money was provided by crowdfunding, using BTC.

The development of Ethereum will see it go through four versions by 2018. There have always been questions about its security and its scalability. During 2016, the DAO (decentralized autonomous organization), a clever set of smart contracts (we say much about these later) created with Ethereum managed to crowdfund $150 million. The worries about the security of Ethereum proved well founded, when a hacker stole $50 million (US) from the DAO. Because of this mishap, the Ethereum community split, leading to two Ethereum. These are Ethereum (ETH), the number two cryptocurrency, and Ethereum Classic (ETC), which has market capitalization of more than $1billion (US) at the beginning of November 2017.

Chapter 2: How does Cryptocurrency work?

Most cryptocurrency, although not all, uses blockchain technology. Blockchain is a revolutionary idea that is changing everything. With blockchain, digital information can be distributed, without there being a danger of having it copied. Originally, blockchain was only used for Bitcoin, which as we have seen is the premier digital currency, however, new uses far beyond those of a financial nature, are continually being discovered for it.

Ledger: Any discussion concerning blockchain, soon mentions *ledger*. What is a ledger ? A ledger is record of financial accounts such as equity, assets, debts, inventory, transactions, liquidity, etc.

GENERAL LEDGER

ACCOUNT ____________ MONTH OF ____________
ACCOUNT NUMBER ____________ NUMBER ____________

DATE	ITEM	TRANSACTION		BALANCE	
		DEBIT	CREDIT	DEBIT	CREDIT

Blockchain is a digital ledger: The block chain is a digital ledger that can be programmed. Not only can it be programmed to keep financial records but it can be programmed to keep records of all sorts of things. It is useful to compare the blockchain to a spreadsheet, duplicated over a network of many computers called *nodes*.

Each node is joined to all other nodes of the network. When a node receives information about a new transaction, checks on this transaction are automatically made; these checks include:

- What is the transaction that the sender proposes?
- Does the sender have the authority to do this transaction?
- Even if the transaction is within the rules, is it possible to carry it out?

Any node receiving information about a transaction can answer these questions with its copy of the blockchain. The node transmits its decision concerning the legality of the transaction to all the other nodes. If a consensus of nodes agree, with a digital mechanism called *proof-of-work*, that the transaction is valid, then it gets recorded in a block.

Regularly and frequently, every 10 minutes, the blockchain is updated. As a consequence, the ledger is never out of date. The blockchain is a distributed database of records. As the blockchain is not stored in a single location, but spread over many computers, corruptibility is minimized because it cannot be interfered with. The records are private, but important encrypted parts on the blockchain, are public and can easily be verified. The information contained on the blockchain is public and up-to-date. Every transaction has a public record on the blockchain and this cannot be altered.

Allow me to continue the spreadsheet comparison. If we are working on a sheet, other users are usually locked out and cannot work on it. However, if we use Google sheets, part of Google Docs, then two or more people can use the same sheet at the same time. A huge amount of time and money could be saved, if all important transactions could involve all concerned parties simultaneously, rather than being passed from point to point, being checked and signed off at each point.

You may think,' Couldn't this system be extended to finance and other important domains?' Currently, Google has that spreadsheet stored in a *cloud* database. That means, whoever owns Google has the final control. Google's motto was,' don't be evil,' and you may wonder why worry? Well, now the owner of Google is Alphabet Inc. who changed the motto to,' do the right thing.' In the end, big companies only care about themselves, despite their wonderful mottoes and slogans.

Blockchain is more than just a big spreadsheet distributed over a network of nodes. The blockchain is a sequence of blocks of information, which is possessed by each node. Blocks are being added to the blockchain all the time, as new transactions take place. If you want to see the Bitcoin blockchain being added to then go to the site *https://blockchain.info/*

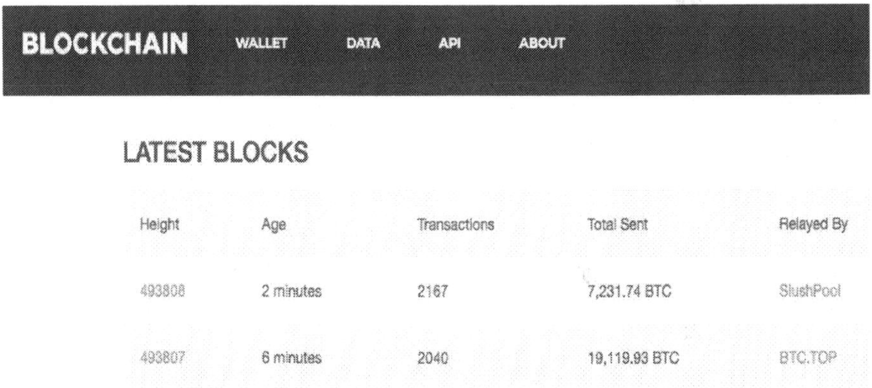

BLOCKCHAIN WALLET DATA API ABOUT

LATEST BLOCKS

Height	Age	Transactions	Total Sent	Relayed By
493808	2 minutes	2167	7,231.74 BTC	SlushPool
493807	6 minutes	2040	19,119.93 BTC	BTC.TOP

If you want to see the Ethereum blockchain being added to, then go to the site *https://etherscan.io/*

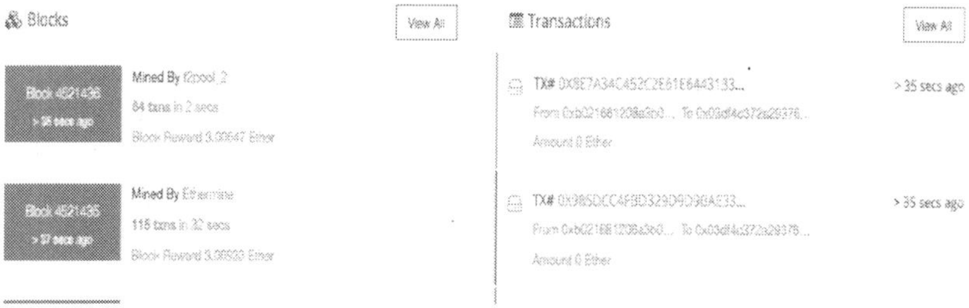

there are other, but less important blockchains, which you can see if you are interested. Special nodes called miners make the blocks. Mining needs very complex problems in mathematics to be solved!

What actually is a block? All transactions are recorded in the blocks.

Blockchain gets its name from these blocks. A block is a file containing data including:

- A timestamp
- A reference, called the *height*, to the previous block.
- The transactions that are recorded within the block .
- A record of the problem that had to be solved by miners.

Block #493808

Summary		Hashes	
Number Of Transactions	2167	Hash	[illegible]
Output Total	7,291.73916513 BTC	Previous Block	[illegible]
Estimated Transaction Volume	1,026.96316673 BTC	Next Block(s)	
Transaction Fees	2.9684473 BTC	Merkle Root	[illegible]
Height	493808 (Main Chain)		

If you have a look at either site mentioned before you will see the word *hash*. This is extremely important but will be dealt with more thoroughly later.

Here is a very simple comparison of how the blockchain works, using people as nodes.

- You have ten people, A,B, C, D,......J, trading among each other, who each have a copy of a ledger called *Blocky*.
- All transactions they do have to be recorded in Blocky. Blocky has many pages, which are called blocks.
- Two of the people, C and H, are allowed to record new transactions in the blocks.
- C and H are the miners.
- In order to free up a new page for recording transactions, C and H have to solve a hard math problem.
- Whoever solves it first, gets a prize.
- Once a problem is solved then the date, a reference to the previous block, records of a whole lot of new transactions and information about the problem are put in the block.
- Information about the new block is transmitted to all nodes.

- The nodes have to agree that the transactions in the proposed block are legitimate.
- There is a vote on each transaction and if everything is OK, then the new block goes into every copy of the ledger. The vote is different to an electoral vote. There is a digital consensus, found by systems called *proof-of-work*, *proof-of-stake* and other names.

This is a very simple comparison of a very sophisticated process, which is changing the world. To be more accurate, we should mention that the transactions are encrypted, that the math's problem to be solved involves all transactions that have ever taken place. There is also the matter of security and the nonce number helps that. The nonce number is another technical term that lay people do not have to know much about. It is discussed more fully later in this chapter.

Summary: A blockchain consists of connected blocks, created by miners and maintained by nodes. Transactions on the blockchain are encrypted. Blocks contain hashes of all transactions that have been confirmed. Miners use unconfirmed transactions to make new blocks. Each time a transaction occurs there is a *nonce* number to maintain the security of the transaction. A hash of any transaction goes in the blockchain once it has confirmed. Confirmation of the transaction occurs once most nodes agree about the validity of the transaction, using the proof of work system or similar.

A crude introduction to the mathematics and computing follows. Do not worry if you cannot understand this. You can greatly benefit from cryptocurrency even without knowing this. Skip it if mathematics and technology leave you cold.

Mathematics and Computing

Encryption: Encryption works like this. If *A* contacts *B* to transact, *B* sends to *A*, usually with *A* knowing, a *public key*. *A* performs the transaction with *B*.

The public key works on the transaction, and produces an indecipherable file. *A* sends this encrypted file to *B*. If a hacker intercepted the file, all they could see is an encrypted and illegible load of rubbish.

On receipt by *B,* a private key acts on the encrypted file enabling *B* to read it.

For the majority of people, they do not need to know the mathematics of encryption. However, if you do then remember high school mathematics and something called *prime numbers*.

Prime numbers have only two *factors*. These are whole numbers that divide into the number without a remainder. Prime numbers can only be divided this way by 1 and the prime number itself. Some very simple primes are 2,3, 5, 13 and 17; 1 and 5 can only divide the number 5, if there is to be no remainder; 1 and 13 can only divide the number 13, if there is to be no remainder; 1 and 17 can only divide the number 17 if there is to be no remainder.

The prime numbers are infinite. This means that no matter how large a prime number you find, there is always a larger one. This is a most important feature of primes and their use in encryption.

All whole numbers are the products of prime numbers. It is easy for a computer to find the primes that are multiplied to give a small number, however, if the number is obtained by multiplying two very large primes then centuries would be needed to find the primes. All encryption is currently based on this property of prime numbers.

Prime numbers create the public and private keys used in encryption. We would need a completely new method of encryption, if computers were much quicker than they are now.

Hash Functions: A hash functions takes data of varying size and changes it to data of fixed size. Here is hashed data on a block of the Bitcoin blockchain

000000000000000000 1b494644d2043868dc7e33f7a58638d be889e194eb2b57

Here is another

a0bd8b7f051ca1a667cceb112433e0e2f01068955ebb2662a6a9 540cddf4dd90

You might note that both these strings have 64 characters. This is interesting, however, not all data is changed to the same length, on the same block, because different hash functions are at work on a block and may have different roles.

How do hash functions fit into the blockchain? Blockchain is comprised of blocks, created by miners solving mathematics problems. They use unconfirmed transactions to create the blocks. The transactions get recorded in these blocks. The transactions are recorded in blocks in hashed form. Any individual will usually find their transactions in different blocks, particularly if their transactions take place at different times.

Any description of the mathematics of the blockchain is not finished, unless *nonce numbers* are mentioned.

Nonce number: When we use blockchain, there is a nonce number for each transaction. The nonce number provides a record of the number of transactions from any particular address (where you're sending data from). Every time you transmit a transaction from this address the nonce number iterates (increases by one). Transactions are placed in blocks in nonce order.

If a transaction has a nonce of 0 then it gets placed before those with a nonce of 1, which in turn go ahead of nonce of 2 etc. This prevents double spending.

A transaction hash has only one nonce number. The reason for this is security. This prevents hacking attacks called *replay attacs*.

That just about covers the mathematics, albeit at a low level, now what about computing. Wikipedia and other references say,

' *Ethereum* is a *blockchain-using platform, which is open-source, public and allows smart contract scripting. Execution of these scripts occurs on Ethereum's network of nodes, using the EVM (Ethereum Virtual Machine). The Ethereum Virtual Machine is a decentralized Turing-complete virtual machine.*' or something along these lines.

The previous paragraph is meaningless to the layperson, just a pile of confusing mumbo jumbo. Don't get too worried, if like the pieces about mathematics, you don't understand. The following is for those who have a technical bent.

Turing-complete: if a computer program or platform can do anything that is programmable, then it is Turing-complete. A word processor is not Turing-complete as it can only produce text.

As far as we know, it is not possible to write a computer program to simulate getting embarrassed, so you could not do that, even on a Turing-complete platform. However, if it was possible to write a program on a platform to do anything, which is programmable, then that platform is Turing-complete.

Apparently, Ethereum is Turing-complete, however, Bitcoin is not Turing-complete. Bitcoin and its underlying language are for financial calculations and transactions only. This is a major difference between Ethereum and Bitcoin.

Ethereum Virtual Machine: A virtual machine is a computer-programming environment. The Ethereum Virtual Machine runs on every node of the Ethereum blockchain. As it is Turing-complete, it can execute any smart contract, which is written on it.

Chapter 3: Pros and Cons of Cryptocurrency

This chapter has a look at the advantages and disadvantages of cryptocurrency.Cryptocurrency is often compared with fiat currencies and stocks of the sort you buy and sell in stock markets. We mentioned earlier that the currencies we currently use in our day to day lives such as dollars, euros, yen, and renminbi are called 'fiat' by the people needing to differentiate them from cryptocurrency.

In spite of the word currency appearing in cryptocurrency, at the moment, cryptocurrencies resemble stocks more than they resemble fiat money. The purchase of a cryptocurrency is not only the buying of the coin, but also the purchase of a type of technology stock and, usually, although not always, an entry in a blockchain.

Has Cryptocurrency Any Advantages Over Fiat Money?

It certainly does so and some of these are listed below.

1. Generally, cryptocurrencies are decentralized and are beyond the control of any nation, bank or business.

2. Due to the supporting network of nodes and miners, cryptocurrency has no central point where failure would spell the end of the currency. Hence if one miner or exchange of bitcoins or other significant cryptocurrencies collapses then the currency continues to exist.
3. Much greater privacy can be obtained by using cryptocurrencies than using fiat currencies.
4. Once someone gets used to them, cryptocurrencies are quite simple to use and often much cheaper than fiat currencies, which usually have significant fees for a lot of transactions.
5. It is much quicker to transfer cryptocurrency than fiat money.
6. If you are a merchant, you do not have the danger of chargeback where an unsatisfied or dishonest customer can cancel a credit card transaction.
7. Due to their digital form, cryptocurrencies are far more robust and portable than fiat money.
8. Because cryptography is used, there is far less chance of fraud than with fiat money, where credit card numbers are often hacked and sold on the Internet.
9. Another frightening possibility with credit cards is financial information, even identity theft, when you give your card to an organization such as a shop or hotel, as your full credit line is exposed. The merchant pulls the

money from your account. Cryptocurrencies work in a different way, you push the money to the merchant. They do not get to inspect your credit line.

10. A very significant advantage of cryptocurrency is the extremely widespread global access to the Internet. There are more than 2 billion people who can access the Internet but can't access traditional exchanges, such as banks. As an example of how important this is, there are African countries, where as many as 30% of the population use Bitcoin.
11. The major cryptocurrencies have universal recognition. If an Australian travels to America, he or she has to change Australian dollars to US dollars, then change back on return home. With Bitcoin, Ether and other significant alt coins, this is not necessary. They are universally recognized.
12. All other moneys are owned or created by someone else. Paypal is a good example of the possible unfortunate consequence of this. If they decide that they want to freeze your account then they can do so, without any consultation with you. It is your responsibility to get access to your funds again. With cryptocurrency, this cannot occur as the money is in your electronic wallet and only you can access that with your keys.

OK, these are the advantages but *are there any disadvantages?*

Here are some, listed below.

1. Bitcoin can handle 7 transactions per second, yet the VISA system can handle as many as 56,000 per second, with an average of about 2,000 and daily peak of about 4,000. This is the scalability problem that Bitcoin must overcome in order that cryptocurrency replace fiat.
2. If the scalability problem is resolved, then extremely powerful computers will have to be miners and these are very expensive. The decentralized nature of the blockchain would be compromised if there were only a few very powerful miners.
3. Many people invest in cryptocurrency, however, all cryptocurrencies are proving to be very volatile with movements of ±5% or more daily. Currently cryptocurrency is not suitable for most people, as anything more than a speculative investment.
4. Hackers are causing serious problems with some major cryptocurrencies. Ethereum, Turing-complete, seems to be particularly vulnerable. In 2016, a Hacker stole $50 million(US) from the DAO(Decentralized Autonomous Organization), an investment fund based on Ethereum. In July 2017, another hacker stole $31 million from a wallet based on Ethereum, and in November 2017, a learner inadvertently destroyed about $200 million (US) of Ethereum funds! These problems will be

resolved, Bitcoin had similar mishaps in its earlier years but seems to be all right now.

5. There are not enough nodes. Those people opting to run nodes seem to do it for idealistic reasons. Idealism is all well and good, but in a world where money talks, it is debatable whether the current situation can continue forever.

Finally we look at the cryptocurrency scene and try and identify those cryptocurrencies among the large number that exist, which offer something of worth.

A useful rule of thumb in assessing cryptocurrencies, is that a cryptocurrency should provide a platform and not just features. What do we mean by a platform?

A cryptocurrency that provides a platform is something more than electronic money, it should provide the means by which this can take place. Some of the many cryptocurrencies do this but are designed for particular markets, such as legal marijuana or gambling.

The assessment of a cryptocurrency should compare it to large and successful cryptocurrency platforms such as Bitcoin or Ethereum. Is the comparison a favorable one? If not then it is doubtful if the coin is a good investment.

The next chapter considers some of the leading cryptocurrencies.

Chapter 4: The most common Cryptocurrencies

An inspection of *coinmarketcap* or one of the other sites showing cryptocurrencies reveals a great many other cryptocurrencies than Bitcoin and Ethereum. These won't all be discussed, however, in the top ten near the middle of November 2017, I found Bitcoin, Ethereum, Bitcoin Cash, Ripple, Litecoin, Dash, Monero, Neo, NEM, Ethereum Classic as the top ten then IOTA. I mention IOTA, as it is a particularly interesting cryptocurrency.

Bitcoin Cash(BCH): On August 1st, 2017, there was, what is called in the cryptocurrency world, a soft fork on the Bitcoin Network. This led to a brand new cryptocurrency, *Bitcoin Cash* (BCC), often BCC is written as BCH. This new currency arose because of major differences in the community of Bitcoin.

The problems leading to this have never been completely resolved and consequently, there was to be what is called a hard fork on the Bitcoin blockchain, called the SegWit2. This hard fork never took place.

In the August 2017 soft fork, anyone in possession of the old coin received the same value of the new coin. There were many who did not want the new coin and attempted to sell them immediately. Whether this was possible, depended on the exchanges they used. There were some exchanges that would not trade in Bitcoin Cash.

Some well-known exchanges such as Bittrex, Kraken, CoinOne, Coinbase , and Poloniex did trade in it and since August 2017, Bitcoin Cash has gone from strength to strength, on November 17, one BCH was worth $1,369, over a 100% increase in one week.

What is all this fork stuff anyway? It concerns the blocks of the blockchain, the tables containing information about transactions. One Bitcoin (BTC) has 1Mb, maximum block size, and as a result only 250,000 transactions BTC per day are possible, **with 7 transactions per second**. Bitcoin Cash(BCC) has a maximum 8Mb block size limit that allows many more transactions per second.

The number of transactions, with this could be about 2,000,000 per day. When you consider that the VISA system is capable of handling up to 56,000 transactions per second, with an average of about 2,000 and daily peak of about 4,000, you see there is a big problem. A problem of scalability that Bitcoin must solve if it is to replace fiat money.

Not withstanding the difference in blocksize, there are not many differences in how you can use the two coins are used.

Ripple: On November 13 2017, Ripple (XRP) was the fourth most valuable cryptocurrency. It is not possible to mine Ripple, as you can mine Bitcoin or Ether. In the cryptoworld, Ripple is almost an old timer, as it started in 2012. Ripple is open source, it is not owned by a company such as Microsoft with Office or Adobe with Photoshop.

Ripple resembles Bitcoin, as its network enables P2P trading and transactions need approval by a distributed network of computers. Mining does this for Bitcoin and Ether. The method Ripple uses is *iterative consensus* and this is different to mining. Reasons for this difference are extremely technical; they explain why you cannot mine Ripple. Iterative consensus allows for transactions that are far quicker and more energy efficient.

There was a proposal to build an XRP network for the creation of smart contracts. This was to be called *codius*. Codius has not gained nearly the same popularity, for this purpose, as Ethereum. Ripple is mainly used for financial settlements. Japan, the third largest economy in the world, accepts Ripple as currency.

Earlier we stated that the number of Bitcoin would never exceed 21,000,000. Similarly, the number of Ripple has a maximum of 100,000,000,000.

Dash(DASH): A cryptocurrency, highly rated as regards privacy and anonymity is Dash. One of the reasons for this is that Dash has *fungibility*.

What is fungibility? A coin has fungibility if a unit of the currency is of equal value in A as in B, its value is independent of location.

One of the reasons for the enhanced privacy and anonymity is that Dash possesses something called PrivateSend, which mixes Dash coins anonymously over different points in its network. There is a feature on PrivateSend that gives Dash less appeal to criminals, and PrivateSend helps maintain fungibility. Fungibility is even better than encryption at maintaining both anonymity and value.

On Nov 13 2017, Dash had capitalization in excess of $4 billion and was ranked about 5th. One DASH exceeded $500 (US), which is more than a doubling of value in two months. It is wrong to confuse Dash with either CoinDash(CDT) or Dashcoin(DSH), which are totally different coins.

Litecoin: Litecoin (LTC) is a child of Bitcoin. On November 13, 2017, Litecoin had market capitalization of more than $3 billion (US) and one Litecoin had a value of $59 (US). It was created by a man called Charlie Lee, who used to work for Google. There can never be more than 84 million LTC. It is quite similar to Bitcoin, but has more features. It is interesting to note that Litecoin has SegWit activated, while Bitcoin just repudiated SegWit. Litecoin is quicker than Bitcoin; Litecoin blocks are produced about four times as frequently as Bitcoin, however, Litecoin is not as secure as Bitcoin. If privacy is an issue then Litecoin is no more private than Bitcoin.

Monero (XMR): Monero is another favorite of those seeking an anonymity-oriented alt coin. Monero began in 2014 and on November 13 2017, was number 7 by market capitalization of cryptocurrencies, with capitalization of nearly $2 billion (US) and 1 XMR worth more than $125 (US). Monero has always put a high premium on very high levels of privacy. In spite of that, a report in 2017 described a serious problem in Monero code; this has been rectified.

NEO(NEO): Neo is a crypto currency, originally called AntShares is, created in China. It has been created to be in sync with Chinese government rulings on cryptocurrency. Like

Ethereum, NEO is a platform, which enables the development of smart contracts. NEO has collaborated with Microsoft to create some of its features. The problem of scalability has been taken very seriously and NEO claims to be able to handle 1000 transactions per second and eventually 10,000! This compares very favorably with Bitcoin's 7 transactions per second, and Ethereum's 15 transactions per second. A particularly useful feature of NEO is NeoFS, which involves the storage of large files on nodes in the NEO network. Security has been taken very seriously and it is believed that even quantum computers, when they become common, will be unable to crack the security of the Neo network. NEO is a cryptocurrency with a market capitalization of more $1.75 billion (US), the value of one NEO is more than $20.

NEM(XEM): NEM (XEM), originated from Japan in 2015. Although cryptocurrency is opposed to banks, Japanese banks have assisted the development of NEM. NEM has a consensus mechanism called *proof- of -importance* rather than the proof-of-stake, which is typical of other crypto currencies. NEM was written using the Java computer language. NEM has inbuilt features that discourage wealth inequality and encourage transactions on the networks. These features have not been addressed, to any large degree, by other crypto currencies. NEM is a cryptocurrency with a market capitalization of more $1.65 billion (US), the value of one XEM is only $0.2.

Ethereum Classic(ETC): Ethereum Classic rounded out the top ten cryptocurrencies, when I checked on the coinmarketcap site in mid November 2017. As with Bitcoin Cash, Ethereum Classic (ETC), a cryptocurrency with a market capitalization of more $1.5 billion (US), resulted from a fork, although this took place on the Ethereum blockchain and not the Bitcoin blockchain. Far more could be said about this however it is sufficient to state that the value of one Ethereum Classic coin was worth more than $15 (US) in mid November 2017.

IOTA (MIOTA): IOTA is very interesting cryptocurrency. It has been specifically created for the Internet of Things (IoT). You could well say,"What is the IoT?" The Internet of Things is the Internet of Everything and involves lighting, infrastructure, gas and just about any appliance. As the IoT becomes a reality then the Internet will feature in all parts of our lives.

Unlike many other cryptocurrencies such as Bitcoin and Ethereum, IOTA does not use a blockchain. In contrast to blockchain, IOTA has no blocks; it uses the Tangle. The Tangle is a very interesting system with a new way of reaching consensus. The Tangle is known as a directed acyclic graph (DAG) in mathematics and computer science. The Tangle is the distributed ledger, stored on the nodes of the network of IOTA. The Tangle will permit the scalability, so very lacking from Bitcoin and Ethereum.

A very interesting facet of IOTA is that it provides protection if there is quantum-computing. Quantum computing is founded on the idea that rather than having only 2 states 0 and 1, there are three states. If quantum computing becomes a reality, then many current encryption systems will be at risk. IOTA, like NEO, has worked to overcome this danger, before it arises. You may recall that this was a feature of the cryptocurrency NEO.

IOTA has a market capitalization of more $1.65 billion (US), the value of one MIOTA is only $0.60.

In addition to these top cryptocurrencies, there are literally hundreds of others. Have a look at the site of coinmarketcap to see many of them.

Chapter 5: Employment in Cryptocurrency

Making money with cryptocurrency

There are several ways of making money with cryptocurrency. Employment is the first, mining altcoins is another, the purchase of some then trading with it is another, and you could invest in ICOs. We will devote the next few chapters to these. This chapter looks at employment.

Employment: If you're talented at programming and mathematics then there are some wonderful jobs in this field. The Indeed Employment site, in late-November 2017, had more than 300 jobs where skills in Bitcoin or cryptocurrency were required, and the salary was $50,000- $150,000 per annum.

Here is an example from the Indeed site that required a strong computing background. The salary offered was more than $85,000(US).

Software Engineer - Crypto/Payments

San Francisco or Remote

Engineering

Full-time

By joining Kraken, you'll work on the bleeding edge of bitcoin and other digital currencies, and play an important role in helping shape the future of how the world sees and uses money. At Kraken, we constantly push ourselves to think differently and forge new paths in a rapidly growing industry fraught with unexplored territory, which is why Kraken has grown to be among the largest and most successful bitcoin exchanges in the world. If you're truly interested in pushing the envelope by disrupting an industry that some say cannot be disrupted, then we just might have the job meant for you. Kraken is a place for dreamers and doers - to succeed here, we firmly believe you must possess each in spades. Check out all of our job postings here https://jobs.lever.co/kraken.

Our Engineering team is having a blast while delivering the most sophisticated crypto-trading platform out there. Help us continue to define and lead the industry.

Responsibilities

- *Integrate our financial systems with blockchain currencies and banks*
- *Integration of user-facing elements developed by front-end developers with server side logic*
- *Writing reusable, testable, and efficient code*

- *Design and implementation of low-latency, high-availability, and performant applications*
- *Implementation of security and data protection*
- *Integration of data storage solutions*
- *Write highly scaleable, high volume services*

Some of the jobs did not require programming or mathematics skills.

Have a look at this.

Direct Sales Rep - Cryptocurrency Specialist

Nexxus Partners - Hamilton, OH

$10,000 a month - Commission

Job Summary

Nexxus Partners is a Bitcoin and Cryptocurrency services company. Nexxus has created solutions to help the average non-techie learn about and use cryptocurrency. One of our ecosolutions brings merchants and shoppers together for a win-win-win for everyone. Nexxus helps small businesses get and keep new customers with an innovative mobile commerce app that lets customers shop at hundreds of local and international businesses, and earn cash-back rewards.

In this position, you'll be connecting with business owners and organizations and present them with our products, build relationships, and close deals in the Nexxus community. This is a lucrative opportunity with a competitive commission-based pay; an average rep can realistically earn around $10K per month, while motivated reps have the *opportunity to earn around $25-50K per month.*

You will not be alone as you will be part of a sales team working together to build a residual income while building the Nexxus network.

If you:

1. are an entrepreneur

2. are self-motivated

3. can work without delegation

4. see that Bitcoin is exploding!

Then let's talk

Job Type: Commission

Required education:

- *High school or equivalent*

so if you're keen to try your hand at a full-time job in this field, there are many openings.

It could be that you prefer freelancing to full-time working for one company, then check this job advertised on Upwork, a site for freelancers:

Hi,

I need a plug-in for Metatrader 4 that will create charts of Bittrex com cryptocurrencies inside Metatrader for each timeframe M1, M2, M5, M15, M30, H1, H4, D1, W1, MN1. I want all the cryptocurrencies listed on Bittrex as Metatrader 4 charts like the charts EUR/USD that is present in each mt4 terminal.

The job consists of:
1 - Creating a bridge allowing to display charts inside of Metatrader, based on Bittrex data / prices/volume. (all instruments / cryptos)
2 - Possibility to send market buy/market sell/limit buy/limit sell orders from inside Metatrader, to be executed inside the Bitcoin exchanges.

I must be able to add indicators on the cart for analysing the cryptocurrency. It can be done using Bittrex API.

I need the source code for modifying it if API changes.

If you have questions, please send me a Message, before bidding.

Thank you.

- ***Project Type:*** *One-time project*

$250

Fixed Price

$$

Intermediate Level

I am looking for a mix of experience and value

November 20, 2017

Start Date

This job was for $250 and would take less than a week, for someone familiar with this type of project. Before embarking on this or something similar, consider the next paragraph.

For the tech sector, if you have excellent skills then consider this. Universally, there is an ever growing lack of talented IT staff, particularly in specific fields that includes cryptocurrency. A Google search for IT freelancing sites will reveal that talented IT people should stay away from online sites as they seek work.

If you use sites like Upwork, then skilled professionals are bidding for jobs against those of poor quality. People prepared to submit low tenders to get appointed. The result of this leads to a race to the bottom, where wages are concerned. Talented people from the West will be competing against people from Third World countries, prepared to work for meager pay and whose work is sometimes of dubious quality.

If you prefer contract type work of the freelance type with a variety of employers, then positions of this kind can be found on sites like Indeed. Here is an example.

Ethereum/Blockchain engineer

Combine Layers - Houston, TX

Full-time, Part-time

Job Summary

We are looking for a senior technical architect/developer who has worked with Ethereum, Ripple or bitcoin blockchain, experienced in solidity programming or any equivalent technology related to blockchain and cryptocurrency development.

Responsibilities and Duties

Understanding business requirements, design and develop organization's technical architecture, managing end to end technical solution, leading developers and development effort within the startup set up, mentor and guide junior developers Conceptualize and develop use cases per business requirements Lead and develop Proof-of-concepts(POC) and Proof-of-Value(POV) Develop 'smart contracts' and programming effort on Ethereum blockchain, develop ERC-20 tokensMonitor and manage cloud servers and other infrastructures/toolsDevelop exciting new solutions with blockchain/hyperledger technologies

Here is another job on Upwork.

Bitcoin & Cryptocurrency Journalist Needed $0.05/word

Article & Blog Writing *Renewed 2 hours ago*

Needs to hire 2 Freelancers

Looking for a professionally trained journalist who can write two (2) 400-800 word daily articles on bitcoin, cryptocurrency and blockchain news topics.

Requirements:
- Choose own topics and work independently.
- Desire to hunt and scoop timely stories.
- Format subheadings and post own articles daily on Wordpress.
- Source and attach accompanying featured image.
- Add correct category and tags.
- Familiarity with and passion for these topics is desired, but not required.

This will be an ongoing gig with opportunity for promotion and increased workload.

Starting pay is $0.05 per word with future raises and bonuses possible.

- ***Project Type:*** *Ongoing project*

Featured Job

$50

Fixed Price

$$$

Expert Level

I am willing to pay higher rates for the most experienced freelancers

November 22, 2017

Start Date

Skills and Expertise

AP Style Writing Chicago Manual of Style Financial Reporting Investigative Reporting Journalism Writing News Writing Style

This job requires journalism skills, with a deep interest in cryptocurrency.

There are hundreds of such gigs advertised on Upwork, and there are many other sites for freelancers.

Content Mills

Until recently, I did not know the term, *Content Mills.* Here is an Internet definition,' *A **content mill** or writers **mill** is a slang term used by freelance writers and given to a company, website or organization designed to provide cheap website **content**, usually at a significant profit to themselves, and usually by paying very low rates to writers.'*

Google searches will produce many articles about content mills. Many are very critical of them, and Upwork is called a content mill. Content mills are often talked about with contempt. If you are very able and desire a freelancing career make sure to read these links:

https://www.thebalance.com/writing-for-content-mills-1360505

http://www.makealivingwriting.com/4-new-content-mills/

http://www.aliventures.com/should-avoid-content-mills/

Chapter 6: Making Money from Cryptocurrency with Mining

What is Mining?

To answer this question, it is necessary to remember what is cryptocurrency. Cryptocurrency is digital money that uses cryptography, the process of changing legible information into an unbreakable code.

The purpose of this is to help track purchases and transfers by keeping them private and anonymous. Cryptography uses mathematics and computer science developed during the World War II as a means of transferring data and information secure from enemy snooping.

In earlier chapters, we saw that most cryptocurrencies run on a blockchain, which is a digital ledger distributed across a network of computers called nodes. The blockchain is updated several times an hour.

All transactions and all ownership of cryptocurrency are recorded in the blockchain. The blockchain is created by miners, who use powerful computers that process the transactions and place them in blocks. Miners are paid for doing this, with the 'coin,' as fees for transactions.

Cryptocurrency mining involves adding transactions to the blocks of the blockchain. Transactions are secured and verified as this is done. This process leads to new currency. Individual blocks can only be added by miners when they contain a proof-of-work or PoW. This means a hard problem in mathematics has been solved.

Mining requires a computer and computer programs, by which miners compete with others to solve these problems. This process involves substantial computer resources. The mathematical problems involve hash functions.

On the Bitcoin blockchain, the reward for mining a block is currently 12.5 bitcoins.

Initially, there were only a few miners. However, as cryptocurrencies increased in value, mining became a lucrative business. In order to mine successfully specialized equipment is necessary.

A complete mining kit has graphics cards, at least one processor, plenty of memory, and other equipment, and would have a cost around $3,000 on Amazon. Two companies dominant in consumer-grade mining hardware are Canaan and Bitmain. Bitmain is based in Beijing and does mining, as well as manufacture mining hardware.

Mining of Bitcoin: Almost certainly the first cryptocurrency that was mined was Bitcoin. The first mining of Bitcoin was in 2009, using a desktop computer. As more people became involved in Bitcoin then so did the number of miners of it. As this took place, it stopped making economic sense to mine Bitcoins in this manner. Simple computers, even those equipped with graphics processing units, are not powerful enough. Mining in this way would cost more in electricity than the return you might get in coins.

The mining of Bitcoins needs specialized machines known as Application Specific Integrated Circuits, ASIC's for short. They fit onto a computer like a graphics card. It is possible to spend a few hundred dollars to thousands of dollars on this equipment.

If you are committed to trying mining, consider the joining of a mining pool. There is a better chance of return on the investment than if you mine alone. Mining pools unite the resources of their members and reward them by the size of their input to the pool.

The diagram below shows the well-known mining pools and their proportion of Bitcoins that are mined.

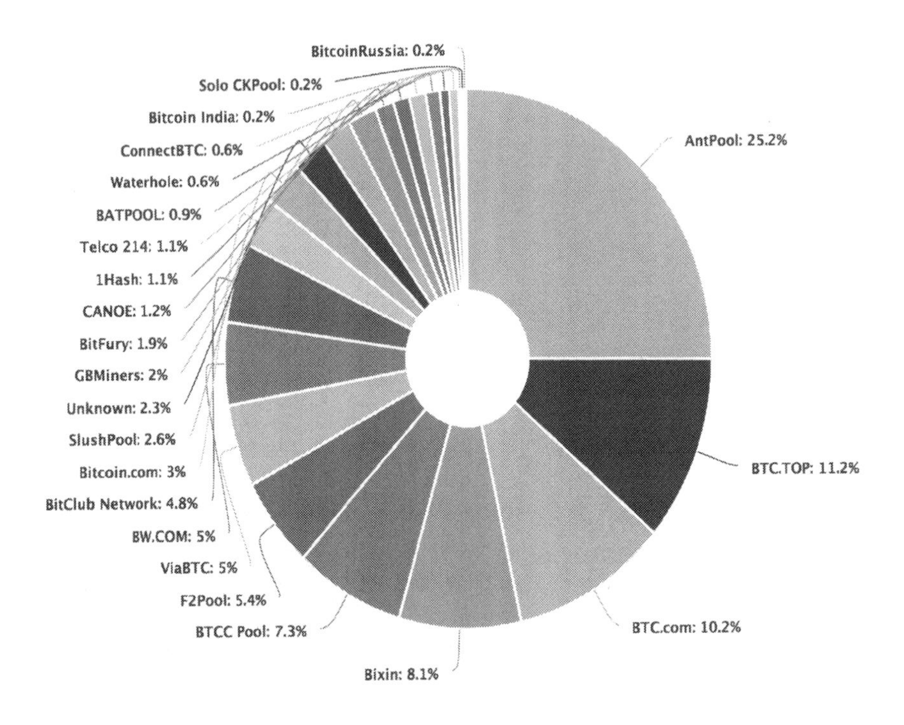

Mining pools are concentrated in China, which boasts of 81 percent of the network hash rate.

Mining of Ethereum: Ether, which is the coin of Ethereum, is mined differently to Bitcoin. There is no mining equipment for the mining of Ether. Ether has been designed to resist mining, with the sort of material used for mining Bitcoin. Ether can be mined with an ordinary desktop computer, but far more efficiently when the machine possesses a GPU. If you want to mine Ether, the GPU should have at least 3 GB of RAM. If you have this, then you still have to install and use some special software.

Think carefully before you start mining Ether. If all you want to achieve is getting Ether, then you will be much better off purchasing them at an exchange dealing in cryptocurrencies. Purchases are much more straightforward and have better returns if you trade in cryptocurrency.

What about the mining of other cryptocurrencies?
We pointed out that some cryptocurrencies cannot be mined. When you visit a site like *coinmarketcap*, you will notice some crypto coins that you cannot mine. However, most cryptocurrencies can be mined. You may question whether it is a sensible thing to do. If you're interested, then it can be areally fascinating thing to do. But as a serious income source then my previous comments about Bitcoin and Ether apply. Some coins can be mined far easier than the big two, and there is a small chance that any coin that you mine will be of great value in the future but don't count on it.

Cloud Mining: For those wanting to be involved in mining another possibility is *cloud mining*. This type of mining is especially useful for those wishing to be involved in mining but are not technically minded and do not want to purchase mining equipment or software. Sometimes, someone who wants to be involved in mining lives in a country, such as Germany, where the cost of electricity is high and as a consequence would find it uneconomic to mine cryptocurrency.

Your first step in getting involved in cloud mining will be to decide the best deal, a 500GH contract, a 1000GH contract or other contract and for how long. The majority of Bitcoin contracts are a year in length. Some are advertised as infinite. However, as most mining equipment will soon be obsolete, this would mean the mining company would quickly be running at a loss. Some cloud miners have Bitcoin or litecoin contracts of lengths from 6 Months to 24 months.

You should carefully consider your needs, and what different cloud miners provide. There are references on the Internet, where you can compare cost per GH and length of contracts. Do a check on any cloud mining company you propose to do business with as there are a lot of cloud mining scams.

The reason that the field of cloud mining produces scams is that it is quite simple to setup a cloud mining website. Having set the site up, it is so easy to make claims that the so-called cloud mining company is an actual mining operation.

The company could seem legitimate by sending proper, initial payments to its clients. However, after that, things go septic, and they keep the payments already received for hash power, and the client receives no more payments from them.

In 2017, at least two cloud mining scams have been outed.These were Bitcoin Cloud Services and HashOcean.The payment method accepted by a cloud mining company is often a clue as to whether they are a scam. Cloud mining companies will accept PayPal, Bitcoin, and credit cards. If a cloud mining company accepts Bitcoins only then it is probably a scam.

You cannot reverse a Bitcoin payment. If you pay the scam company in Bitcoin payment, then there is no chance of retrieving way your coins. Another hint of a scan is a free trial. There is **No** legitimate company giving away free cloud mining. This is equivalent to the distribution of free money. If you find a company giving trials, which are free, particularly if they ask for payment details, then you are probably dealing with a scam.

Another thing you have to be careful of is cloud mining viruses. Some viruses infect computers and then use the victim computer to mine for Bitcoins or other cryptocurrencies. If you believe you have been subject to such an attack, then use a malware detector.

There are some legitimate cloud mining companies. Two of them are Hashflare and Genesis Mining. I suggest you obtain your first cloud mining contract with one of them.

Some people confuse cloud mining with mining pools. They are two different things. In cloud mining, you let someone else do the mining while you just invest in them. You cannot join a mining pool without mining equipment.

Chapter 7: Trading in Cryptocurrency

Trading in cryptocurrency: Cryptocurrency is receiving a considerable amount of publicity. This has arisen mainly from the fantastic rise in the dollar value of Bitcoins, Ether, and other altcoins.

In 2017, the value of one Bitcoin (BTC) has risen from around $1,000 in early January to over $8,000 in November. Ether has done also done well throughout 2017. During November 2017, one Ether was worth around $450 per coin. In Jan 2017 one ETH had a dollar value around $8; this exceeds a 5000% rise!! If only we had invested then!

Unfortunately, investments in altcoin are not always so rosy. In June 2017, at one exchange at least, the value of 1 ETH fell to less than $0.10(US)! Fortunately for those who had a lot of ETH, the dollar value of 1 ETH, by late August 2017, rose again to greater than $350.

This brings us to you. Should you invest in cryptocurrency? There are a lot of commentators on the Internet that think you should make such an investment. As far as they can see cryptocurrency will always have an increasing value. Cryptocurrency is compared to the situation of desktop and laptop computers. In the 1980s it was thought by some discredited experts(?) that personal computers had no future.

History has shown they were utterly wrong. Anyone who was wise enough to invest in what are now technology giants, such as Apple, Hewlett-Packard, Microsoft, and Dell, who were all starting then will have laughed all the way to the bank.

Some words of advice before investing in any cryptocurrency, learn as much as you possibly can. There are many who failed to realize that you cannot assume the value of an asset will always increase just because its value is rising at present. History is full of examples of substantial increases that are followed by even higher falls. This foolish belief caused the recent economic crisis of 2007-2008 that there could be no collapse in property values after an extended period of growth. The reasons that values seem to rise forever may be deliberate lies, complete incompetence, and massive exaggeration.

Please heed this warning, before rushing into the purchasing and trading of cryptocurrency. If you are determined to start then start with *exchanges* specializing in cryptocurrencies. These exchanges make it possible to buy cryptocurrency with fiat money. You will need to do this initially unless some kind person has given you some BTC, ETH or another altcoin.

Good exchanges will help you begin and should be delighted to assist you with the advice you might need, before taking the plunge and starting to trade in cryptocurrency. Thoroughly investigate an exchange before doing business with them.

When an exchange has personnel, who are unable or unwilling to answer questions, and display arrogance, ignorance or both, then take your business elsewhere.

Fortunately, there are some terrific exchanges for those who are beginners at trade in cryptocurrency. Among those in the USA are Coinbase, Kraken, and Cex.io. Sometimes in another country, you could find the country is only just beginning or hasn't even started in cryptocurrency. Despite this, there are usually one or more local exchanges that will help you. Always be sure to check them out carefully though.

Some exchanges only deal with the significant cryptocurrencies such as Bitcoin, Ether, and Litecoin. Generally, after selecting an exchange, you have to fill in some forms. This is a legal requirement before they can accept you. They are required to do this to ensure you are legitimate and not some money launderer or another criminal. You have to do this before you begin trading.

You should get experience with the big coins, such as Bitcoin and Ether, before trying some of the more mysterious ones.Once you have this experience and want to try something more exotic, then Bittrex and Poloniex are exchanges that can assist with smaller coins. In some countries, there may be difficulties in getting smaller coins.

When you start, finding some trustworthy person to assist you to begin is a great blessing. There are many resources on the Internet, such articles, blogs, forums and Youtube videos, on every feature of trading in cryptocurrency. You must take great care as it is so easy to make mistakes. Never forget that if you lose your cryptocurrency, it is gone forever.

There is a final point that should be made about cryptocurrency, and that is the use of *bots* for trading.

Bots are automated systems for sharing information, answering queries and performing actions, such as trading altcoin for money and vice versa. A good example is *Haasbot*, a trading bot that is popular among some cryptocurrency traders, which does the majority of the required tasks for its users. Haasbot watches prices and exchange rates. It trades and even does more.

Bots are used in many other fields besides cryptocurrency. As they are very efficient, it is possible that you have interacted with a bot without knowing this was happening. Many bots require a subscription to use them. In some cases, it is possible to subscribe in this way with Bitcoin.

Bots are based on AI or artificial intelligence. Bots improve their performance by using machine learning. The more people interact with bots and use them for more and more tasks, the more the bots learn. The creation of such bots is at the cutting edge of modern technology.

To generate income in cryptocurrency, you need to pay attention to what is happening on the market. Shifts in the market can occur very quickly, and you can lose money, by not acting soon enough, or not having the time to trade at the right time. For this reason, what is called trading bots have become popular.

Usually, in the past, you needed time, knowledge or skills for really successful trading. It is possible to dabble and earn some money, but not a substantial amount, without you being a very active participant on a full-time basis. As a result of bots, you can be involved in the trade of cryptocurrency, while focusing elsewhere.

At the very least, there are bots available that can answer your queries. These bots will make it easier to trade. They can provide cryptocurrency updates. The abilities of bots go up from there. You can use them to look up recent trends and inform you what others are trading and the amounts traded. It is possible for bots to provide all the resources necessary to be a successful and active trader.

But what effect is the having on the cryptocurrency industry and market? The widespread use of bots is making trading more competitive, and it is one of the reasons for the boom in cryptocurrency. Arbitrage trading, which means the buying of commodities in one market and selling them for higher in another is a possibility with bots. Bots can also be used in *market making*, which means making profits that arise from long-term sales and orders.

There are many such bots available. Among them are Haasbot, Tradeware, Zenbot, Cryptotrader, and Gecko; to name a few.

Although there are numerous possible benefits, there are also risks, and these must be borne in mind. Always remember that bots are a tool, NOT a complete solution. It is up to you to have the final say; to select the trade. A bot can only focus on a trade you pick. Pick wrong and lose money!

Chapter 8: Making money from Cryptocurrency with ICOs

ICOs: The acronym, ICO, represents *initial coin offering*. An ICO is like an IPO (initial public offering), with the critical point of difference that IPOs are much more closely regulated than ICOs. As cryptocurrency becomes more mainstream, then regulation will probably strengthen.

As stated before, Ethereum and some other blockchain platforms produce smart contracts that do far more than merely transfer digital currency, even though this role is crucial. Most of these blockchain projects claim to improve considerably or entirely replace traditional processes. Some of these blockchain projects do this. However, there are some using blockchain for no other reason than using it. When this happens, the project usually improves nothing.

It is up to the prudent investor to choose those that meet a real need and to avoid the others.

What are the characteristics of an outstanding smart contract? When the blockchain is used for no other purpose than showing clever features, it has probably been designed to confuse naive investors. These projects rarely provide a platform for further developments. What is meant by platform? It is a smart contract offering different services.

At the moment, there are lots of smart contracts, both created and on the drawing boards. Sadly, only a few meet a real need. Most smart contracts do not provide good long-term investment. Bitcoin and Ethereum have set the standard for blockchain projects. Evaluate ICOs by comparing what is on offer with Bitcoin and Ethereum.

Why ICOs? A company gets funds from investors during an ICO, so that the project can be developed. An ICO features a coin or token for sale; investors purchase this token, generally with ETH or BTC. Sometimes they can buy them with fiat currency.

Websites such as *Coinschedule* or *ICOALERT* show the massive number of ICOs.

What happens during an ICO? If you go the site Coinschedule; you will see a lot of ICOs. You can use cards, list, and plates to scan these ICOs.

Usually, when you click on an ICO, the first thing you see is the company's logo followed by a short description of the project. After that, there should be a list: beginning with Project type and leading to Whitepaper. The whitepaper is extremely important for investors in an ICO. If you are a potential investor, then analyze what the whitepaper is saying. An excellent whitepaper reveals essential facts about the project. Do not even think about investing in an ICO without understanding what you must look for in a whitepaper.

- The whitepaper should give a straightforward and concise overview of the project and what the project will do.
- Check how advanced the project is. Many have not gone beyond a vision of what the project might do.
- Is there source code on Github or some other reputable site. This code is essential for you or your computing people to see the coding of the project.
- What about a prototype or working model? If a project lacks a working model, there is nothing to show it might work.
- Is there a market for the product? The whitepaper should talk about this.
- What are the tokens (coins) for sale designed for?
- The whitepaper should show how token holders can make money.
- If there are bonuses or bounties, this should be stated in the whitepaper.
- The whitepaper should reveal any hard cap or soft cap.
- A hard cap is the maximum number of coins that will ever be available.
- The soft cap is different to the hard cap. A soft cap is the minimum number of coins that need to be sold for the ICO to be a success.

- A fundamental question for investors is *escrow*. Escrow protects investors so that their invested funds are returned if the ICO fails.
- A whitepaper should be very detailed about the team developing the project. These people should be carefully checked on Google, social media, forums, etc..
- The whitepaper should analyze the competition. Do not just take what the whitepaper says at face value, as the whitepaper may be lying. Do your research about how much competition there is and whether the project could meet this competition.
- Does the proposed product or service provide something new, worthwhile and realistic?

For example, let us examine HADE, an ICO, which runs November 21, 2017, to December 1, 2016.

Project type Token, Platform Ethereum

Here the introduction says:

Platform for individual investors, finance professionals, and financial institutions with triple-digit revenue, traffic, and active user growth that combines information technology with powerful applications in data visualization & analytics, machine learning, and artificial intelligence.

Their whitepaper is 46 pages long.

I went through it looking for the points I stressed before:

- Project overview and Project outcome. **Both these were covered.**
- How advanced is the project? **A website, whitepaper, and database of the information of 4,500 companies have been created. More than this was not easily seen.**
- Source code on Github. If lacking, then maybe they have not thought about coding for the project. **No material on Github was found under the name HADE. No code?**
- Is there a working model? Don't invest in a project without a working model. **I found no working model.**
- The whitepaper should realistically discuss the market for the product. **This possible market is described well.**
- The whitepaper should state what the tokens (coins) for sale are designed for. **This whitepaper does this well.**
- It should be obvious how token holders can make money. **One service will be to analyze ICOs. If true then this would undoubtedly be of use. There were promises of free services, services that are quite expensive with competitors**

- Information about bonuses or bounties should be precise. **These are clearly spelled out.**

Essential questions the whitepaper should answer are about hard cap and soft cap.

- The hard cap of an ICO is the maximum number of coins. **For HADE it is 1000,000,000**
- The soft cap of an ICO is the number of coins that must be sold for the ICO to be successful. **I could not find this.**
- What about *escrow*? **None mentioned.**
- Team? **Six people are mentioned in the white paper.**
- Competition? Do not just take what is said in the whitepaper as gospel as the whitepaper may not be truthful. Find out how much competition there is and how ready the project is for this. **The competition was identified as Bloomberg, Reuters, and Ycharts. The claim was made that what HADE offers is superior and cheaper than the offerings of the competition.**
- You must check and find out if what is being offered provides something new, worthwhile and realistic. **Their whitepaper claims that the use of Artificial Intelligence makes what they do superior to the competition. A careful check by**

any potential investor that this was true would be essential.

This quick analysis reveals that before you invested in this ICO, you would need much more scrutiny. I am not dismissing it out of hand, and a more thorough investigation may show it to be really good.

In summary

The majority of people want quick returns on their investments and ICOs seem to promise these returns. As we said before, at the moment ICOs have not got the regulatory framework of other investments. When there is no regulation, it does not take long for criminals to appear, making all manner of promises for riches and unfortunately ICOs are a great temptation for those who are dishonest.

The SEC (Securities and Exchange Commission) has warned investors considering ICOs to take care about such investments. Promises of amazingly high returns, offers not sought, things to good to be true, a pressure to buy without delay are all signs of fraud.

What proportion of your investments should be in cryptocurrency? Stories, where people made fortunes with small investments in cryptocurrency, are correct. However, never forget that cryptocurrency is very volatile. For significant returns in this asset, you have to manage your investments actively. If you are a beginner then start small, maybe $100, and only use this until you are confident you can handle more. Do not be in a rush.The younger you are, the higher proportion you can invest in cryptocurrency and ICOs. Talking about ICOs, ***unless you know an industry well and can see how some smart contract project on offer could be of benefit then forget about them.***

Chapter 9: How to Store and Cryptocurrency

Storing Bitcoin and other cryptocurrencies are executed with *wallets*. A 'wallet' for cryptocurrency is a secure, digital *container* for the storage, sending, and reception of Bitcoin and other altcoins.

A wallet is not a purse of the sort shown above. It is a type of software. Most cryptocurrencies have an official wallet. Some of the better-known coins have officially recommended third-party wallets. You must have a wallet, or several, to use cryptocurrency.

Wallets have keys, but not the type that is shown above. They appear as the following

0x4d22459d6712b4599346734cac066de375c76e20

A digital key is a long string of characters. These allow you and no one else to use your wallet.

Are Cryptocurrency Wallets Secure? Wallets have variable security. If you only possess a small amount of Bitcoin or other cryptocurrencies, then you can take some risk. However, if you have a large sum then get as much security as possible. When your guard is down, hackers strike.

Some wallets use bio information in addition to other measures for security. Another security feature, which is worth having, is multi-signature transactions. As with anything to do with software, you must back up wallets. You should also encrypt your keys.

At the very least one backup should be located on an external hard drive of some type that has no Internet connection. Make sure, if disaster strikes, you can retrieve your funds. Disasters could include the accidental erasure of your computer's hard drive or perhaps the theft of your computer.

If your wallet or your keys are lost, then you can say goodbye to any cryptocurrency within it! A Golden Rule never has more currency in a digital wallet than you can bear to lose.

Here are some well-known sorts of wallets

Desktop Wallet is the most frequently used type of wallet. Usually, it is an app that is connected to the coin's client. Wallets are available for all major computer operating systems. An excellent example of a desk wallet is the Jaxx wallet, made by Decentral, which has Windows, MacOS and Linux versions as well as a Chrome addon.

Mobile Wallets are wallets equivalent to desktop wallets that run on a smartphone app. Often they are mobile versions of desktop wallets. For instance, Jaxx has wallets for both iOS and Android.

Online Wallets are as their name suggests online wallets. One advantage of such wallets is that you do not have to download or install them. The wallet resides in the 'cloud.' Some have encryption features, allowing for the encryption of coin before going to the wallet. As with anything online, such wallets are not as secure as those that are offline.

Hardware Wallets are usually USB like devices for the secure storage of Bitcoin and other cryptocurrencies. They are designed to convenient and are recognised as the best method of storing cryptocurrency.

Paper Wallets. These are QR codes for both public and private keys that you print. The use of these with your cryptocurrency is quite simple, once you are used to this method of storage. If you use them, then it is vital to back your keys up in some other way. Keys like this are very flimsy, and even such ordinary things as a cup of coffee, a strong wind, a cat or child with a pen is a serious threat.

It is quite simple to move Bitcoin or some other cryptocurrency from an exchange to a wallet. The following example uses the exchange Coinbase and KeepKey, which is a hardware wallet:

- The KeepKey USB cable is plugged in.
- The KeepKey wallet is opened.
- The wallet address is found on the User Interface of the KeepKey Client.
- The Coinbase 'Send/Request' tab is clicked on, and the KeepKey wallet address is entered(Use a copy and paste of this, unless you have an extraordinarily good memory).

- Follow any instructions then complete by clicking 'Send Funds.'

Until you are used to this, usually it is prudent to send only a small sum first to be sure that all is all right before sending the rest of the money, if the sum to be sent is considerable.

The rest of this chapter describes the MyEther wallet for the Ethereum currencies.

Bitcoin(BTC) is the premier cryptocurrency. It has the largest market capitalization of more than $130 billion(US), with one BTC worth more than $8,000. Ethereum(ETH) is the second highest ranked cryptocurrency with corresponding values of more than $35 billion(US), with one ETH worth more than $350.

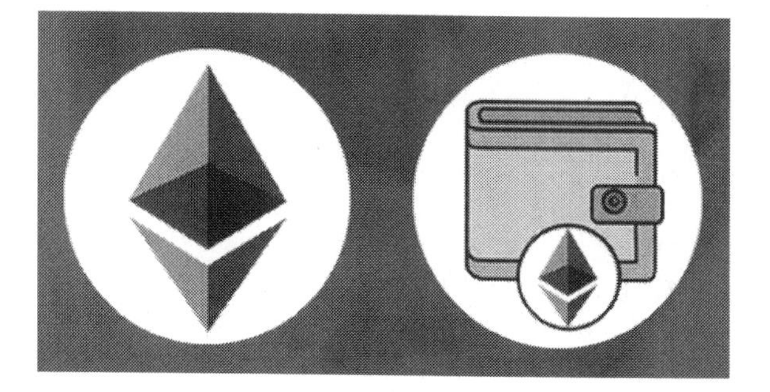

An excellent article about Ether storage can be found at the link https://coinsutra.com/best-etherum-wallets/

The MyEtherWallet is one of the wallets recommended in this report.

The MyEtherWallet (MEW) is an entirely free, open source software for creating wallets to work with the Ethereum platform. You should be aware that there are transaction fees if you send ether, but those fees go to the miners working on the Ethereum blockchain and not to MEW. These fees are minimal and nothing in comparison to the fees you pay a bank for similar services.

The MyEtherWallet is a brilliant, simple and flexible solution for ETH and other digital assets produced with the Ethereum platform.

Which cryptocurrencies can be stored in a MyEther Wallet?

The following can be stored. Note that MyEther Wallet is only of use for Ethereum. It cannot be used to store Bitcoins.

- Ether (ETH)
- Ethereum Classic (ETC)
- Any standard Ethereum token (ERC-20) issued on the Ethereum platform

Ready to start?

Begin on the link https://www.myetherwallet.com/

MyEtherWallet

Create New Wallet

Enter a password

Create New Wallet

Already have a wallet somewhere?

It is a good idea to read *Getting Started*. You start with a neat diagram, which shows in a very rudimentary way what is happening on the blockchain.

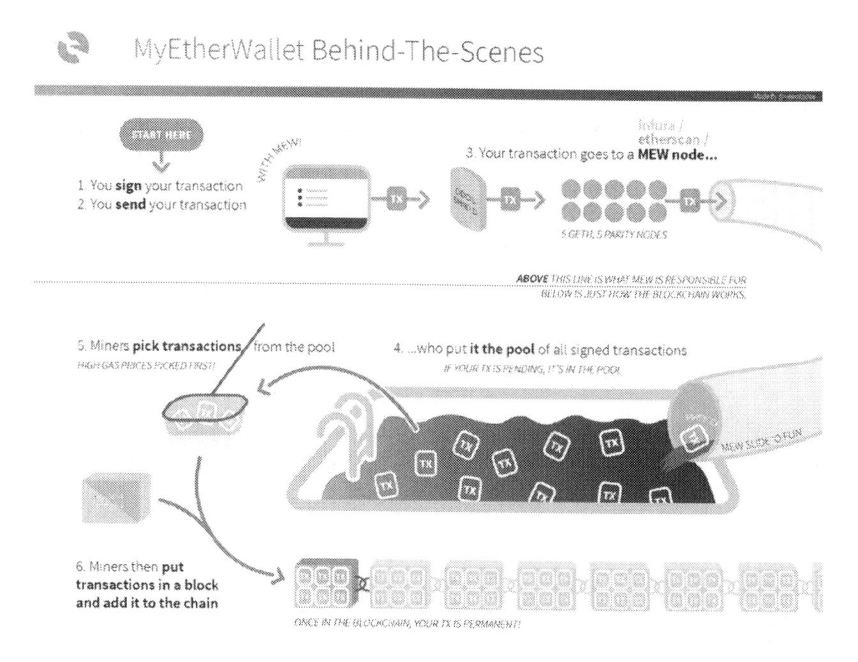

This is probably only of interest to geeks and others worried about the technical details. You do not have to understand this to get, store and use Ether, the coin of Ethereum.

For the technically minded this information is essential.

As well as a web browser, MyEtherWallet is compatible with:

- Geth (a type of software associated with Ethereum)
- Mist Wallet
- MetaMask Wallet
- Jaxx Wallet
- Ledger Nano S hardware wallet
- TREZOR wallet

The final instructions are comprehensive.

How To

1. Create a new wallet.
2. Back up the wallet.
3. Verify you have access to the wallet.
4. Transfer funds to the wallet.
5. Check your balance safely

You can see the various operations you can perform, which are:

1. Create a new wallet.
2. Back up the wallet.
3. Verify you have access to the wallet.
4. Transfer funds to the wallet.
5. Check your balance safely

There is essential information on this page that needs comment.

MEW is a client-side interface that interacts with the Ethereum blockchain. This means that by use of MEW, which is software on your computer that interacts with your browser, you can perform the five operations described.

Although you can quickly create new wallets in your web browser with MEW, it's not an online wallet. The wallet is on your computer, not on the Web! Thank goodness. Otherwise, hackers would have an easy time stealing your funds.

Even though you create the wallet through the web, all of your information and your funds are stored on your computer, not on the MEW servers. They emphasize that MEW does not have the assets. You do, on your computer.

The first operation leads to full instructions about setting up a wallet. This process can also be set in motion by clicking on the button *How to create a wallet* on the welcome page.

Here is a simplified version of what is on this page.

- Go to https://www.myetherwallet.com/.

- Enter a password, as below

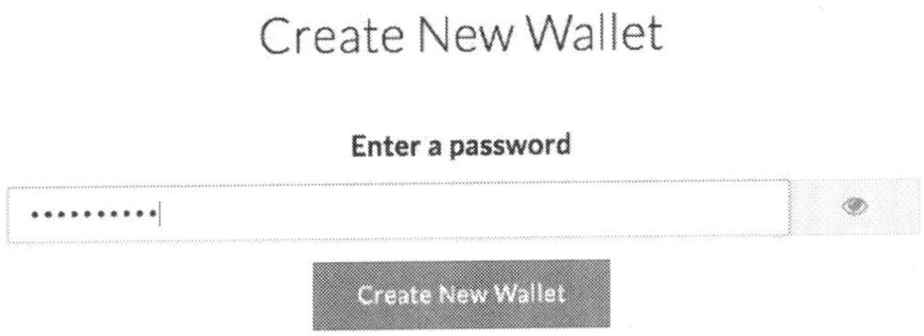

- Click on the *Create New Wallet*

- This brings up this window.

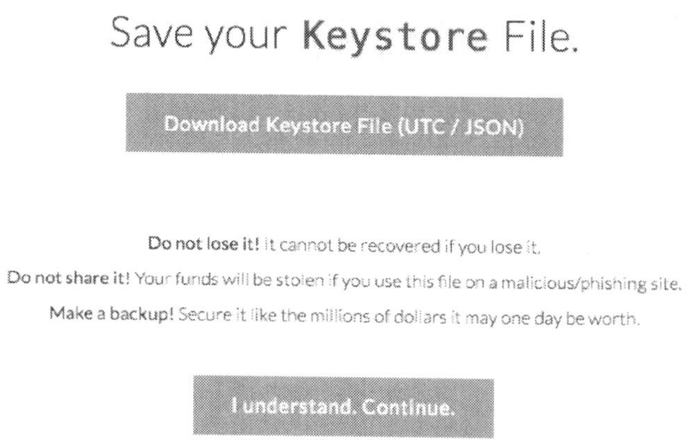

Save your **Keystore** File.

Download Keystore File (UTC / JSON)

Do not lose it! It cannot be recovered if you lose it.

Do not share it! Your funds will be stolen if you use this file on a malicious/phishing site.

Make a backup! Secure it like the millions of dollars it may one day be worth.

I understand. Continue.

- Click on *Download Keystore File*
  - I use Firefox browser and got

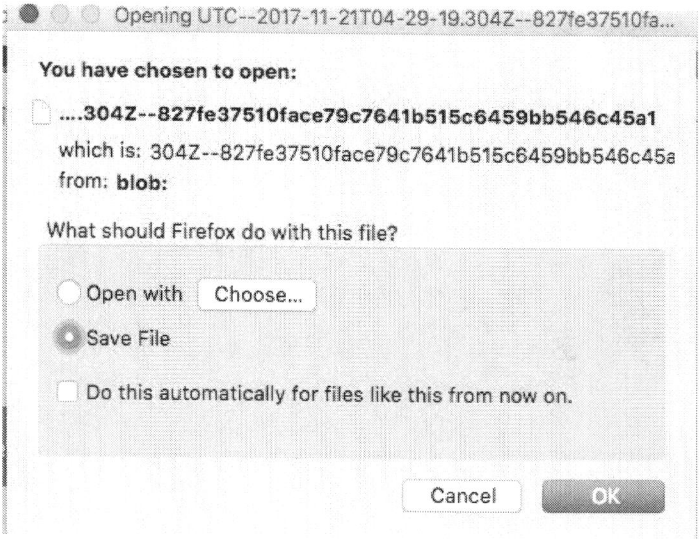

Opening UTC--2017-11-21T04-29-19.304Z--827fe37510fa...

You have chosen to open:

....304Z--827fe37510face79c7641b515c6459bb546c45a1

which is: 304Z--827fe37510face79c7641b515c6459bb546c45a

from: **blob:**

What should Firefox do with this file?

Open with Choose...

Save File

Do this automatically for files like this from now on.

Cancel OK

- Click OK
- Now click *I understand. Continue*

Save Your **Private Key**.

5a604b2be6391674c4728a200eca03632703b85d9ad05f9da58481d95416664c

Print Paper Wallet

Do not lose it! It cannot be recovered if you lose it.

Do not share it! Your funds will be stolen if you use this file on a malicious/phishing site.

Make a backup! Secure it like the millions of dollars it may one day be worth.

Save Your Address. →

- Click *Print Paper Wallet*

- Print this and put it in a safe place.

- Click *Save your Address*, and you will get the window below.

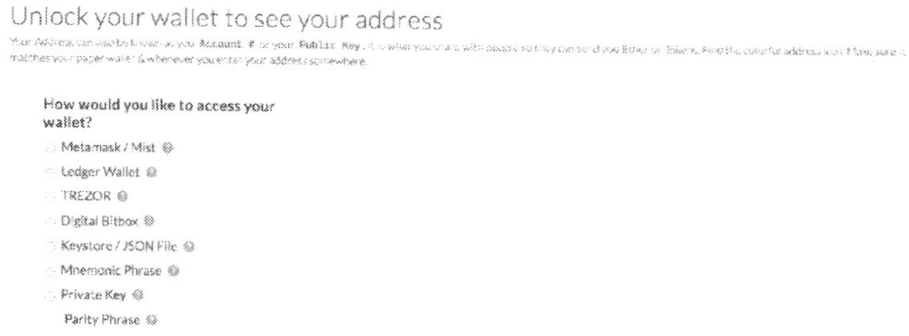

Unlock your wallet to see your address

How would you like to access your wallet?

- Metamask / Mist
- Ledger Wallet
- TREZOR
- Digital Bitbox
- Keystore / JSON File
- Mnemonic Phrase
- Private Key
- Parity Phrase

At this point, you have done everything you can do yourself. If you have never used Ether before, you need to be shown how to obtain some. Good cryptocurrency exchanges should go out of their way to help you do this.

The instructions will be very similar to those given before for *KeepKey* and *Coinbase*.

Chapter 10: The Future of Cryptocurrency

There is a massive number of articles and books that predict a bright future and others that predict doom and gloom. Many of the pieces concentrate on Bitcoin. However, their ideas apply to the entire cryptocurrency world.

In late November 2017, one article in a blog was along both these lines: *What of the future for Bitcoin? The use of Bitcoin has many benefits and will almost certainly retain its popularity as a currency. By volume, the majority of transactions involving Bitcoin occur in China. Hence you can deduce that Bitcoin's future and China will be closely aligned. China is an extraordinary country with many talented people and ancient civilization. As China rises so, Bitcoin will rise also.*

The most significant threat Bitcoin has is that it is replaced or has its functions performed by some of the many other cryptocurrencies. There are some who do not see this as a problem. Bitcoin was the first cryptocurrency, and for that reason, Bitcoin will always exist as a widely used cryptocurrency. There are some who say that this is entirely wrong. They argue that despite Bitcoin being used for making payments, only a small percentage of all Bitcoins are used in this way.

The principal use of Bitcoin is its value as a store of value. If other currencies start to enjoy equal popularity, there will be serious problems for owners of Bitcoin.

Is Bitcoin the 21st-century gold? Does Bitcoin lack the problems caused by the storage of gold? It has undoubtedly been significantly increasing in value since it started in 2009. These trends are good, but will they continue? Perhaps, Bitcoin could just be a fad that will soon be exposed as an illusion. Only time will tell. We just don't know, what's going to happen in the future.

Another found at another site was more negative and went like this: *The crypto bubble can be likened to the dot.com bubble in the 1990s. All cryptocurrencies can be placed in three categories (i) Cryptocurrencies that are seen as value stores, with significant uses in trade and speculation. Bitcoin fits into this category, as do such altcoins as Monero and Litecoin. (ii) The second type of cryptocurrencies are platforms from which Smart Contracts or Dapps can be made such as*

Ethereum predominantly but also NEO and Stratis. (iii) The actual Dapps themselves such as Tenx, Publica, and PIVX.

The author sees strong resemblances between ICOs and the IPOs of the 1990s. During that time, the very word ***Internet*** *had an almost magical effect, fast forward twenty years and now the magic word is* ***blockchain****. Then, sensible people said that just because there was some vague connection between something and the Internet did not mean there was anything more than rubbish involved. The Internet was not a panacea!*

The writer sees something similar happening today, in the frenzy of speculation in anything associated with blockchain. Bitcoin receives far less criticism than many other altcoins and their re ICOs. Often, ICOs are described as stockmarkets for people purchasing hot air, with the thought they may sell it for even more.

This author thinks there is going to be a crash in what is seen as a crypto bubble, just like the crash in the dot.com bubble of 2000. When this crash occurs, regulations will be brought in leading to a 90% reduction in value of good cryptocurrencies and the total demise of most of the lesser. Bitcoin will continue, but it is unlikely one Bitcoin will have its enormous dollar worth that it currently enjoys.

A final article paints a more realistic scenario. Here is a précis of what it said, ' *Experts agree that the current mania of ICOs and cryptocurrencies is unsustainable. Even such celebrities as Floyd Mayweather, the world champion boxer, and Paris Hilton, the now almost unknown blonde whose romantic adventures were an internet hit, have invested in ICOs.*

If something is going to be valuable, then it has to be scarce, but there is no scarcity of ICOs. Most of the cryptocurrencies, which have arisen from these ICO's are based on Ethereum. Ethereum has been around since 2015 and will probably see out this mania. To harness the real value of blockchain and other cryptocurrency technologies, such as that beneath Ripple and IOTA, it is necessary for the current bubble to burst.

Once it has, then we will indeed see the real value of these technologies. In the past one of the drivers of this technology was the desire to free us from the large companies, governments, and banks that dominate our lives. The proponents of this technology believed that we did not want this domination and would be happier without it.

In fact, we probably do want these large organizations in our lives. In response to something so obvious, such large companies as J.P. Morgan and Amazon have utilized blockchain technology. They realize that they cannot turn a blind eye to something that has been designed to replace them. It was naive to think they would just wait to be overthrown.

They have bottomless pockets and what they come up with will probably be brilliant and to the public's liking and will be eagerly embraced, and blockchain will lose its glamour but realize its actual value.

Three articles, three expert writers, three very different views of the future. Where does it leave people like us, as we ponder what the future of the cryptocurrencies will be? In ten years we will know the answers to these questions. Time alone will tell. While the future unfolds, I urge you to be very careful. Greed usually comes before a fall and the crypto bubble will explode just like every other bubble has.

Conclusion

This brings to an end this introductory book about cryptocurrency.

This book has attempted to show how cryptocurrency has the potential to be as important as the Internet.

The book has demonstrated how this amazing technology is so important.

There has been a lot of discussion about this.

There are a number of ways you can be involved and these have been discussed.

There are many reasons to make the decision to invest in it but take great care as you do and proceed with caution slowly.

Good luck in your cryptocurrency future!

Dear Reader,
Thank you for buying and reading my book!
If you like it, please, leave a review. It is important for me and my future books.
Just scan this QR code and you can leave a review

Or just type this link–
https://www.amazon.com/review/create-review?ie=UTF8&asin=B077SP34ZK#

Made in the USA
Lexington, KY
01 June 2018